SPACE!

JUPITER

GEORGE CAPACCIO

Marshall Cavendish
Benchmark
New York

Marshall Cavendish Benchmark
99 White Plains Road
Tarrytown, New York 10591
www.marshallcavendish.us

Library of Congress Cataloging-in-Publication Data
Capaccio, George.
   Jupiter / by George Capaccio.
      p. cm. — (Space!)
   Summary: "Describes Jupiter, including its history, its composition, and its role in the
solar system"—Provided by publisher.
   Includes bibliographical references and index.
   ISBN 978-07614-4244-8
   1. Jupiter (Planet)—Juvenile literature. I. Title.
   QB661.C37 2008
   523.45—dc22
   2008037276

Editor: Karen Ang
Publisher: Michelle Bisson
Art Director: Anahid Hamparian
Series Design by Daniel Roode
Production by nSight, Inc.

Front cover: A computer illustration of Jupiter
Title page: An image of a volcanic eruption of Io, one of Jupiter's moons.
Photo research by Candlepants Incorporated
Front cover: Chris Bjornberg/ Photo Researchers Inc.
The photographs in this book are used by permission and through the courtesy of:
Super Stock: Digital Vision Ltd., 1, 8, 14, 15; Pixtal, 58. Getty Images: James Stevenson,
4, 5; Gary S Chapman, 10; 34, 43; Time & Life Pictures, 31, 45, 50; Antonio M. Rosario,
56. Photo Researchers Inc.: Detlev van Ravenswaay, 17; Shigemi Numazawa / Atlas Photo
Bank, 22; Mark Garlick, 25; Science Source, 53. Alamy Images: Science Photo Library, 21.
NASA: JPL, 26; JPL/University of Arizona, 30; JPL/Cornell University, 32; 46, 48, 47;
http://juno.wisc.edu, 54. AP Images: NASA, 28, 36, 37, 52, 57; George Frey, 41. The Image
Works: Hervé Champollion / akg-images, 38; SSPL, 39.
Printed in Malaysia
123456

CONTENTS

1

THE FIRST OF THE GAS GIANTS

Until the sixteenth century, most people thought Earth was the center of the **Solar System**. In their view, the Sun and the other planets revolved around Earth in **orbits** that were perfect circles. Stargazers of the past were sure the Sun made one complete orbit around Earth each day. It is not hard to imagine why people once held this view. After all, the Sun rises in the east and sets in the west. Also, Earth seems to stay in one place without ever moving. No matter how hard we try, it is impossible to feel our planet spinning on its **axis** as it travels around the Sun.

Early astronomers like Johannes Kepler and Nicolaus Copernicus challenged the Earth-centered view of the Solar System. Their observations convinced them that the Sun was

Jupiter is the largest planet in our Solar System.

really the center. These scientists argued that the planets, along with their moons, were in orbit around the Sun. This might seem like a commonplace observation to people living today. But in the 1500s, this was a shocking notion that threatened people's sense of their place in the universe. If Earth was just another planet circling the Sun, then maybe humans were not so special after all.

Copernicus's view of the Solar System has shaped scientific thinking for more four centuries. According to this model, the Solar System is composed of the Sun, the planets and their moons, and smaller bodies like **asteroids** and **comets**. Since Copernicus's time, scientists have discovered new planets and new moons. Even with these discoveries, people have tended to see the Solar System in terms of levels of importance. Planets come first because they are the biggest. Moons are second, and interplanetary objects, such as comets and asteroids, are in third place.

However, new data from spacecraft are giving scientists an even deeper understanding of how our Solar System works and what it is made of. Nowadays it is becoming harder to classify certain types of objects in our Solar System. For instance, some moons are as large and **geologically** active as some planets. These moons are more like asteroids than they are like other moons. Some asteroids are so icy they are more like comets. And some **meteorites** contain pieces of both comets and asteroids.

Even the difference between a star and a planet is becoming harder to define. We know that stars produce heat and light through reactions in their cores. Planets cannot do this because they are too small. They can only shine by reflecting light from a star. But what about Jupiter? This giant planet gives out more energy than it receives from the Sun. So where is this extra amount of energy coming from? The latest studies show that Jupiter is generating its own heat, which is coming from inside the planet as a result of gravitational force. So in some ways, Jupiter is like a star. If the planet were about eighty times more massive, reactions would take place in its core as a result of the increased pressure and heat. Energy would be released in the form of heat and light. In other words, the planet Jupiter would begin to shine, taking its place in our Solar System as a second Sun. New discoveries and better understanding of the Solar System will continue to introduce more intriguing questions and answers.

PLANETS IN THE MAKING

More than 4 billion years ago, a giant, spinning cloud of gas and dust—called a nebula—began to collapse on itself. Particles of matter close to the center of the cloud interacted more rapidly as the force of gravity increased. The temperature in the center of the cloud kept increasing. Eventually, the temperature became so hot that **atoms** of hydrogen began to fuse together. When this happened, the core of the nebula had become an independent source of heat and light. In other words, it had become a star. We call this star the Sun.

The collections of stars in outer space may be remnants of past galaxies and nebulae, or they may have the potential to become new solar systems in the future.

The cloud, or nebula, was all that remained of much older stars that had burned out billions of years ago and left behind only dust. The dust was mostly microscopic bits of water ice, iron, and other solids. The gas was largely hydrogen and helium. The cloud formed a kind of disk that continued to swirl around the newborn Sun. Over the next million years or so, the dust grains began to clump together as they bumped into each other.

Have you ever made a snowman? One way to start is by rolling a snowball in the snow. As layers of snow build up, the original snowball becomes large enough to make the head or body of your snowman. A similar process takes place when tiny bits of dust clump together in outer space. The bigger the clumps become, the more likely they are to smash into other bodies and take on more material. In this way, tiny bits of dust, spinning around a star, slowly turn into rocky nuggets. One theory of planetary formation suggests that after millions of years, these nuggets grow into planetesimals, or rocky objects that can later form planets. Because of their greater size, planetesimals are even more likely to collide as they orbit the Sun. When collisions happen, the planetesimals either break apart into smaller chunks or increase in size from the build-up of material. Planetesimals will keep growing until they have used up all the raw, or unused, material in their orbits. When this happens, the process is complete and the resulting structures—often planets—cannot grow any larger.

As dust, rocks, and gases continuously collided with each other and moved around, planets and other celestial bodies were formed.

The process of planet formation is not a neat, orderly progression from particles of dust to full-size planets. It is messy and unpredictable with no guarantee that a planet will result from all this smashing and clumping together of orbiting fragments. But this is how planets are formed. Even planets as huge as Jupiter start out as tiny grains of dust and molecules of gas.

THE BIRTH OF JUPITER

Once our Sun had begun to shine, the surrounding cloud of gas and dust began to cool. Molecules of heavier elements turned into solid particles. The nature of these particles depended on how close or far away they were from the Sun. In regions close to the Sun, mineral grains were more likely to change. In the next, or middle zone, carbon-based materials and soot formed. In the outermost zone, furthest from the heat of the Sun, ice became the most common material.

When they reach a certain size, dust grains tend to travel toward the star in the center of the cooling nebula. The bigger they grow, the faster they spiral inward. Incoming dust grains from the icy outer regions of the nebula pile up at what scientists refer to as the snow line. The snow line in our Solar System is the dividing line between the rocky inner planets and the outer gas giants. It falls roughly between Mars and Jupiter. A gas giant like Jupiter will form close to the snow line in most solar systems because this is where there is the highest concentration of hydrogen and helium gas. Some dust grains break through the snow line. Made of solid substances like iron and other metals, they will go on to form **terrestrial**, or land- or rock-based, planets. In our Solar System, Mercury, Venus, Earth, and Mars may have begun as microscopic grains of solid substances.

The growth of Jupiter seems to have followed a different course. Once this planet reached the size of Earth, its powerful **gravity** began to attract greater and greater amounts of gas as it orbited the Sun. The formation of Jupiter made it possible for other giant planets to form. Without Jupiter, there would have been no Saturn, Uranus, or Neptune. Jupiter accumulated so much raw material in its orbital path that it created a kind of gully or channel. Dust grains and planetesimals spiraling inward from the outer regions of the Solar System could not cross this barrier. Instead, they piled up along the outer edge where they gradually joined together to create a new planet. In the case of our Solar System, this new planet was Saturn.

While Saturn is a gas giant like Jupiter, our Solar System's other giant planets—Neptune and Uranus—are more accurately described as ice giants. As Jupiter and then Saturn were forming, they soaked up much of the available gas. They also pushed any remaining planetesimals into the outer regions of the solar nebula. The build up of these planetesimals led to the formation of Uranus and Neptune. Compared to Jupiter, these two planets have much less gas in their atmospheres. However, since they are so far from the Sun, their interiors contain a great deal of ice.

Mercury, Venus, Earth, and Mars are the terrestrial, or land, planets. Jupiter, Saturn, Uranus, and Neptune are considered gas giants, though Uranus and Neptune are sometimes called ice giants. Pluto, which was once considered a main planet alongside the others, is now known as a dwarf planet.

2

THE STRUCTURE AND PHYSICAL FEATURES OF JUPITER

If there were no Jupiter, there would probably be no life on Earth. Scientists think that Jupiter's powerful gravity captures many incoming comets and asteroids that would otherwise have crashed into Earth. However, during the Age of the Dinosaurs millions of years ago, scientists believe a massive asteroid did manage to crash into our planet. The collision raised up tons of dust, material, and other debris that cast a life-threatening cloud over much of Earth. The cloud blocked the sunlight, lowered global temperatures, and may have led to the extinction

This is an enhanced satellite photograph of the gas giant Jupiter and four of its sixty-three known moons.

of thousands of species of plants and animals, including the dinosaurs. Fortunately for us, such collisions are rare, and their rarity may be a direct result of Jupiter's influence.

While Jupiter played a part in allowing life to survive on Earth, it limited the size of its neighbor, the planet Mars. Mars is about half the size of Earth. Like the other terrestrial planets inside the snow line, Mars accumulated rocky material as it circled the Sun. However, Jupiter cleared away much of this material from the orbital path of Mars. As a result, Mars was unable to grow any larger. There just was not enough "stuff" left for Mars to pick up. Jupiter's irresistible gravity also kept another planet from forming between Mars and Jupiter. Instead of a planet, the space between them is filled with asteroids.

JUPITER AND EARTH

Hydrogen and helium are two of the lightest and most abundant elements in the universe. They made up about 98 percent of the original solar nebula, which was the birthplace of the Sun and planets. Like the Sun, Jupiter is mostly composed of hydrogen and helium. Because the planet is so massive, its gravity is strong enough to keep these lighter gases from floating away. Since Earth is much smaller, its gravity is too weak to hold on to them. During Earth's formation, the hydrogen and helium floated off into space. While Earth's atmosphere has continued

Billions of years ago, Jupiter (shown in the center) and other orbiting planets continued to pick up dust, rocks, gases, and other materials that added to their size and composition.

to develop as the planet ages, Jupiter's atmosphere has stayed about the same since its beginning.

Scientists think that Jupiter may have begun as an Earth-size seed or planetary embryo that slowly accumulated gas. The best way to picture this is to think of how cotton candy is made. A large heated bowl melts and blows around thin threads of sugar. A paper cone is twirled inside the spinning bowl. Threads of the crystallized sugar stick to the sides of the cone. The layers of sugar keep building up until a puffy cloud of cotton candy forms. Similarly, as Jupiter spiraled around the Sun, its gravity pulled in huge amounts of hydrogen and helium. In the process, it swelled in size, becoming the largest planet in the Solar System. Saturn,

Neptune, and Uranus—the other giant planets—are many times larger than Earth, but they could never reach Jupiter's size. When those planets formed, there was not enough gas in the more distant regions of the nebula. As a result, those planets did not collect as much gas as Jupiter, limiting their sizes.

Jupiter, the fifth planet from the Sun, is a huge ball of turbulent gases. It is so big it could easily hold all of the other planets in the Solar System. It would take eleven Earths, lined up side by side, to equal the diameter of Jupiter. In terms of mass, which is a measure of how much matter something contains, Jupiter is 318 times more massive than Earth. It contains more than two times as much matter as all the other planets combined. In terms of volume, which measures how much space something occupies, 1,300 Earths could fit inside of Jupiter. Jupiter's largest moon, Ganymede, is almost half the size of Earth.

THE STRUCTURE OF JUPITER

Scientists have observed Jupiter through telescopes as well as from **satellites** orbiting the Earth. The United States' space program has sent six space **probes** to Jupiter beginning with *Pioneer 10,* launched in 1972. In 1995 the *Galileo* spacecraft, which is in orbit around Jupiter, sent a probe deep into the planet's atmosphere. The probe sent back a wealth of data before it was crushed by the planet's tremendous atmospheric pressure.

COMPARING JUPITER AND EARTH

	JUPITER	EARTH
DISTANCE FROM THE SUN	483,800,000 miles (778,600,000 kilometers)	92,957,130 miles (149,600,000 km)
DIAMETER	88,846 miles (142,984 km)	7,926 miles (12,756 km)
AVERAGE SURFACE TEMPERATURE	-166 degrees Fahrenheit (-110 degrees Celsius)	60 degrees Fahrenheit (15 degrees C)
SURFACE GRAVITY	2.36 times Earth's gravity	
LENGTH OF YEAR	11.86 Earth years	365 days
LENGTH OF DAY	About 10 hours	24 hours
NUMBER OF MOONS	49 named; 14 numbered	1
COMPOSITION OF PLANET	Hydrogen; hydrogen-helium atmosphere; ice	Mostly metals and rock
ATMOSPHERE	Mostly hydrogen and helium with small amounts of methane, ammonia, water, hydrocarbons, and other gases	Mostly nitrogen and oxygen

Thanks to more than three decades of research, we now know a great deal about the largest planet in our Solar System.

On Earth, the land, the sea, and the atmosphere are distinct from each other. We can stand along the seashore, feel the sand beneath our feet, hear the waves rolling in, and smell the salt in the air. Things on Jupiter are very different. The planet's interior structure does not have clearly defined layers or zones like we find on Earth and the other terrestrial planets. Instead, one region gradually merges into another. If a spacecraft were able to survive Jupiter's extreme pressure, it might not find any hard surface on which to land. The planet's atmosphere just keeps getting thicker and murkier, turning at last into liquid hydrogen and liquid metallic hydrogen.

Atmosphere

Jupiter's atmosphere consists mostly of hydrogen gas, about 86 percent. Helium makes up about 14 percent of the atmosphere. There are also traces of water, ammonia, various hydrocarbons, and other chemicals. Hydrogen combines with these elements and chemicals like sulfur and phosphorous to create multicolored clouds at different heights. The clouds' shape and color are constantly changing. Lighter clouds are found in what astronomers call zones. Darker clouds are arranged in stripes, or belts. Winds blowing up to 400 miles per hour (600 km per hour) keep these belts in high-speed motion.

Images taken by satellites and spacecraft have shown scientists that the swirled colors seen on Jupiter are actually clouds shaped by the planet's strong storms.

JUPITER

The brown, yellow, red, blue, and white clouds are the giant planet's most visible feature and make up its only known surface. The colors indicate the altitude, or height, of the clouds. Orange-red clouds are the highest. Below them are white clouds, with the highest white clouds made up of frozen ammonia crystals. Further down are brown and gray clouds. Blue clouds appear in the lowest layer of clouds. They can only be seen through gaps in the clouds above. Astronomers have so far not found any clouds made of water vapor, like the clouds here on Earth.

As on Earth, the temperature rises as you go down further into the atmosphere, toward the planet. In 1995, the *Galileo* space probe plunged about 62 miles (100 km) into Jupiter's atmosphere and measured atmospheric pressure and temperatures. On top of the clouds, the temperature is about -230 degrees Fahrenheit

Based on observations and scientific evidence, artists have constructed ideas of what Jupiter's cloudy, gaseous atmosphere is like.

(-145 degrees C). The sky is bluish, and the pressure is about what it is on Earth at sea level.

Below the cloud tops, atmospheric pressure is about ten times greater than it is on Earth. The temperature is a comfortable 70 degrees Fahrenheit (21 degrees C). If there is life on Jupiter, it would most likely exist at this level of the atmosphere. Any life-forms would have to be airborne since the planet has no solid surface this far below the clouds.

Jupiter's colorful, ever-changing clouds float on top of the planet's atmosphere. The cloud layers combined may only be about 30 miles (50 km) deep. Below the clouds, there is a much thicker layer of hydrogen and helium. This layer is about 13,000 miles (21,000 km) deep. Within this region, extreme atmospheric pressure slowly compresses the hydrogen gas into liquid hydrogen.

An Ocean of Liquid Metallic Hydrogen

Going deeper toward the core of the planet, liquid hydrogen, under even greater atmospheric pressure, changes into liquid metallic hydrogen. The **mantle** that surrounds Jupiter's core is an ocean of liquid metallic hydrogen. This ocean is about 25,000 miles (40,000 km) deep. The deepest part of any ocean on Earth is at the Mariana Trench, a valley in the floor of the Pacific

Ocean. The bottom of the Trench reaches a maximum depth of about 7 miles (11 km) below sea level.

Liquid metallic hydrogen is able to conduct electricity. Jupiter's powerful magnetic field may be the result of this electrically charged hydrogen and the planet's rapid spin rate. Jupiter makes one complete rotation on its axis every ten hours. It is the fastest spinning planet in the Solar System. Its rotational speed causes the middle of the planet to bulge outward. Jupiter's diameter at the equator is about 7 percent larger than at the poles.

Jupiter's Core

Below the ocean of liquid metallic hydrogen, Jupiter may have a solid core. If one exists, it would be roughly the size of Earth but many times more massive. The core is most likely made of rock and ice, although some scientists think it may have the density of thick, super hot slush. The core's temperature could be as high as 55,000 degrees Fahrenheit (about 30,000 degrees C). That is hotter than the surface of the Sun! The core's intense heat may be a result of Jupiter's tremendous mass. Computer studies suggest that the planet is squeezing itself tightly together. This ongoing compression releases a great deal of heat. In fact, Jupiter radiates more heat than it receives from the Sun. This heat travels upward through Jupiter's atmosphere and passes through openings in the cloud cover. Astronomers call these openings "hot spots."

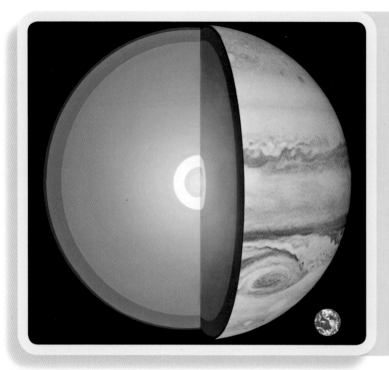

Scientists think that Jupiter might have a central core of solid rock and ice. Layers of liquid metallic hydrogen and gases surround the core, making the planet a gas giant. Giant Jupiter's core is about as big as all of Earth (bottom right).

FASCINATING FEATURES

The Great Red Spot

In 1665, Giovanni Domenico Cassini an Italian astronomer, observed a large, reddish-brown marking on Jupiter. This was the first time anyone had noticed this unique feature. It has come to be known as the Great Red Spot. Jupiter has many storms raging in its atmosphere, but the Great Red Spot is the giant planet's largest storm. It is most likely a hurricane of violently churning gases. The Spot may also be the oldest storm in the Solar

The Great Red Spot is one of Jupiter's most distinctive features.

System. It has been going on for more than 300 years. This monster storm shows no sign of letting up.

From north to south, the storm stretches about 7,750 miles (12,400 km). From east to west, it covers about 14,400 miles (23,000 km). Its diameter is nearly twice as wide as the diameter of Earth, which is about 7,926 miles (12,756 km) at the equator. The storm does not stay in one spot. It travels east and west but never to the north or south.

The Great Red Spot also spins counterclockwise. This movement is the result of two wind currents flowing in opposite directions. A western wind along the northern edge and a slightly slower eastern wind along the southern edge keep the Great Red Spot turning. The heat rising up from Jupiter's core supplies the storm with an additional source of energy. A third source is the smaller storms the Great Red Spot absorbs as it wanders east or west. The Spot's reddish color probably comes from chemicals carried upward on rising heat waves.

Lightning

On Earth, a bolt of lightning is hotter than the surface of the Sun. On Jupiter, lightning bolts are about ten times more powerful. *Voyager 1* and *Voyager 2*, launched in 1977, were the first spacecraft to spot flashes of lightning among Jupiter's clouds. In 2001, while on its way to Saturn, the *Cassini* spacecraft captured images of lightning storms on Jupiter's dark side. In 2007, a National Aeronautics and Space Administration (NASA) spacecraft called *New Horizons* was heading for Pluto and photographed lightning on Jupiter's north and south poles. Until then, no polar lightning had been seen on Jupiter. It was only known to occur on Earth.

Before the *New Horizon*'s **flyby**, scientists thought that most lightning strikes occurred in Jupiter's northern hemisphere. Images sent back from *New Horizons* showed about the same number of strikes in both hemispheres. Lightning has also been detected at Jupiter's equator. On Earth lightning occurs in clouds containing icy water. The same appears to be also true on Jupiter. Warmer temperatures in the lower levels of Jupiter's atmosphere may allow some water to exist. This water could be forming thunderclouds, which are creating lightning storms.

The Rings of Jupiter

While Saturn has the most spectacular ring system in the Solar System, its giant neighbor Jupiter also has rings, though they are harder to see. The innermost ring starts about 55,000 miles (92,000 km) from Jupiter's center. The outer edge of the rings is about 150,000 miles (250,000 km) from the planet.

In the 1970s, NASA's *Voyager 1* and *Voyager 2* spacecraft came close enough to get clearer images of the structure of Jupiter's rings. Photographs from onboard cameras showed a flat main ring, a hazy inner ring called the **halo**, and what appeared to be an even fainter outer ring.

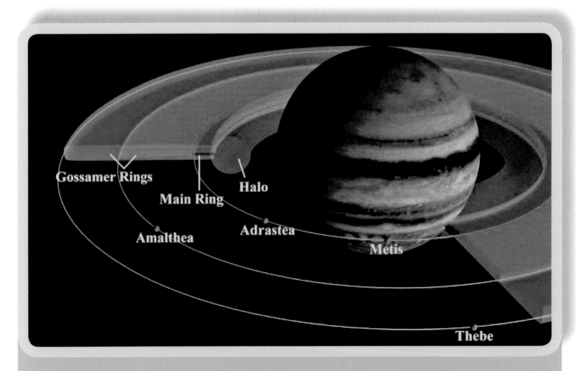

Four of Jupiter's smaller moons (Amalthea, Adrastea, Metis, and Thebe) are most likely responsible for the planet's ring formation.

In 1998 NASA's *Galileo* spacecraft discovered how these rings are formed. Meteoroids, asteroids, and comet fragments crashing into Jupiter's four small inner moons explode beneath the surface of these moons. The explosions send clouds of dust particles into space. These particles are traveling with so much force they escape the moons' gravity and become rings circling Jupiter.

The *Galileo* spacecraft also showed that the barely visible outer ring, called the **gossamer**, is actually made of two transparent rings, one inside the other. *Galileo*'s cameras did not actually see a meteoroid or another object hitting one of Jupiter's four small inner moons. However, the images sent back to Earth clearly showed the craters caused by such collisions. They also showed that the rings of Jupiter are made of the same substance as the surface of the moons—a dark red dust that looks like soot in the rings.

Jupiter's Moons

Jupiter has sixty-three known moons. Some are named, and others are identified by numbers. The four largest moons are Io, Europa, Ganymede, and Callisto.

Io

Until the *Voyager 1* and *Voyager 2* missions, which occurred in the 1970s, scientists knew of only two places in the Solar System with active volcanoes—Earth and Venus. The *Voyagers*, however, discovered that Io had active volcanoes. The spacecraft observed nine eruptions during their trips around Io. Hot, flowing lava on Io continually fills in craters from the impact of meteorites and asteroids. *Voyagers'* scientific instruments helped scientists understand why Io is so active. The reason has to do with Jupiter's powerful gravity. On Earth, gravity from the Moon and the Sun causes the oceans to rise and fall. Water levels rise during high tide and fall during low tide. A similar effect occurs on Io even though the moon has no oceans. So how can a waterless body, like Io, have tides? Jupiter and its three other large moons constantly pull at Io. Sometimes they pull on the same side of Io. At other times, they pull on different sides, depending on their orbits. The combined force of their gravity causes Io's solid ground to swell and sink, just like oceans on Earth. Tidal bulges on Io can reach a height of about 98 feet (30 m). That is several times higher than the highest ocean tides on Earth.

This constant kneading produces heat inside of Io. The moon's interior gets so hot that solid rock turns into molten lava. The lava then tries to escape through the moon's crust.

Images of Io, taken by the *Voyager* spacecraft showed a cratered surfac and volcanic activity. A volcanic eruption is show on the left in blue.

Voyager I was able to transmit fascinating images of Jupiter's four largest moons: Io (top left), Europa (top right), Ganymede (bottom left), and Callisto (bottom right).

JUPITER'S FOUR SMALL INNER MOONS

Europa, Ganymede, Callisto, and Io are called the Galilean moons after the Italian astronomer Galileo who first spotted them in 1610. Four smaller moons orbit the planet inside Io's orbit. Scientists call them the ring moons because dust and rocks from their surfaces are what make up Jupiter's rings. The names of the ring moons are Metis, Adrastea, Amalthea, and Thebe.

Metis is 25 miles (40 km) in diameter. Its orbit is only about 79,500 miles (128,000 km) from Jupiter. It is located inside Jupiter's main ring. Adrastea is about 12 miles (25 km) in diameter. It is the smallest of the ring moons. It orbits 112,700 miles (181,300 km) from Jupiter. Amalthea is the largest of the ring moons with a diameter of about 117 miles (189 km). Amalthea's orbit takes it 112,700 miles (181,300 km) from Jupiter. Thebe's diameter is 60 miles (100 km). Its orbit is 130,000 miles (222,000 km) from Jupiter. Thebe is the outermost of the four small ring moons.

Images taken by the *Galileo* spacecraft compare the size of Amalthea (right), one of the planet's ring moons, to Io (left). Amalthea's shape and size are a result of strong impacts from asteroids and other celestial bodies.

That is why Io has so many active volcanoes. Plumes of sulfur and sodium from some of them have risen about 200 miles (300 km) into space. Volcanic plumes on Earth, by contrast, only rise a few miles. Some scientists think that Io's hot volcanic gases may crystallize in outer space and come down as snow. But snowflakes on Io would be made of sulfur, not frozen water vapor.

Europa

Europa's surface appears blue and white and has many dark, criss-crossing lines. *Voyager 2* showed that the moon's blue and white colors are the result of a thick shell of ice. The dark lines are actually cracks between areas of ice. Instruments aboard *Voyager 2* also picked up signs of a saltwater ocean beneath the ice. This discovery led scientists to think that some forms of life might exist in Europa's ocean.

Ganymede and Callisto

As part of their mission, the *Voyager* spacecrafts surveyed Jupiter's two other moons—Ganymede and Callisto. Their instruments showed that Ganymede is the largest moon in the Solar System. It would be a planet if it were on its own and not held in orbit by Jupiter's gravity.

Images of Callisto revealed a heavily cratered surface. On Callisto, where there are no volcanoes to fill the craters with lava, the craters remain visible even after millions of years. About the size of the planet Mercury, Callisto has more craters than any other body in the Solar System.

A Powerful Magnetic Field

The region in space that contains a planet's magnetic field is called the **magnetosphere**. Jupiter has the largest magnetosphere in the Solar System and the most powerful magnetic field. Scientists think that Jupiter's spinning mantle of liquid metallic hydrogen may be the source of this powerful field. In fact, the planet's magnetosphere is the largest object in the Solar System. It generates enough energy to provide electricity to ten major cities in the United States.

Jupiter's magnetosphere is so large it could easily hold the Sun. On the side facing away from the Sun, the magnetosphere stretches as far as Saturn. The side facing the Sun repels most of the **solar wind**, which is a constant stream of electrically

An image taken by the Hubble Space Telescope in 2000 shows a glowing aurora (blue) wrapped around Jupiter's North Pole.

charged particles from the Sun. On Earth many of these charged particles are trapped in our planet's magnetic field. They interact with gases in the upper atmosphere to create colorful light displays called **auroras**.

Jupiter's magnetic field also creates auroras. On Jupiter these dazzling effects are many times larger and brighter than Earth's. According to one researcher, "Jupiter has auroras bigger than our entire planet." The *Voyager 1* spacecraft first spotted auroras in 1979. At that time, observers had no idea of just how powerful Jupiter's auroras really are. *Voyager 1's* cameras only captured the visible light portion of the auroras. The most breathtaking display was invisible to the human eye.

In the 1990s special cameras were able to reveal the true size and power of Jupiter's auroras. Unlike Earth, Jupiter does not need the Sun's solar wind to create these effects. The planet's speedy rotation generates about 10 million volts of electricity around its poles. When charged particles interact with these high-voltage fields, auroras are born. Some of the particles come from the Sun, but most of them come from Io, one of Jupiter's four largest moons. Io has many active volcanoes, and sulfur and other gases from these volcanoes become electrically charged. Falling into Jupiter's magnetic field, molecules of charged gas give rise to brilliant auroras around the planet's north and south poles. Besides being many times more powerful than auroras on Earth, the bright lights of Jupiter are always glowing.

3
EXPLORING JUPITER

Long before the invention of telescopes or the age of space exploration, many people knew there were other planets besides Earth. The word "planet" comes from the Greek language and means "wanderer." To ancient observers of the heavens, the five known planets were wandering objects. Unlike stars, the planets shone with a steady light and changed their positions throughout the year. The largest of the known planets seemed to rule the night sky. The ancient Romans called this planet Jupiter, their name for the king of gods. It is a fitting name for the largest and most powerful planet in our Solar System.

Nobody knows exactly when Jupiter was discovered. However, scientists and historians do know that the Italian astronomer Galileo discovered Jupiter's four largest moons. In 1610, he

A NASA drawing shows what *Pioneer 10* would look like when it passed by Jupiter in 1973.

In Greek mythology, the king of gods was known as Zeus. However, the ancient Romans' king of gods, Jupiter, was used as the official name for the largest and most powerful planet in our Solar System.

spotted four objects hovering near the planet. He saw that these four objects were moving along with Jupiter. After several weeks had passed, Galileo realized they were actually moons in orbit around Jupiter. Many scientists think that Galileo's discovery was one of the most important in the history of astronomy.

Galileo published his findings in a book known in English as the *Starry Messenger.* Religious authorities who read Galileo's book thought his ideas went against religious teachings. This did not stop Galileo from continuing his scientific work. But a rival astronomer, Simon Marius, claimed that he had discovered the moons of Jupiter one month before Galileo. The question over which man had been the first to spot these moons became one of the earliest controversies involving Jupiter. Simon Marius might have been right. But because he did not publish his findings until much later, the credit goes to Galileo.

However, Marius gave names to Jupiter's four largest moons. Galileo had wanted to number them I through IV, using Roman numerals. In 1614 Marius came up with names from mythology. He called three of the moons Io, Callisto, and Europa. These were the names of three Roman goddesses or nymphs. Jupiter, the lord of the gods, was supposed to

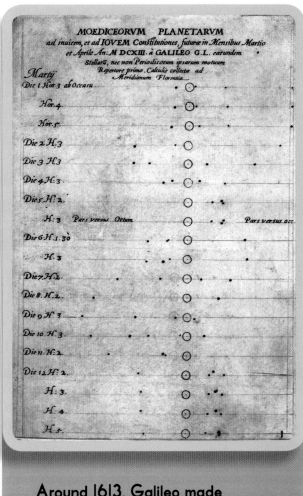

Around 1613, Galileo made these drawings to show his observations of Jupiter's moons.

have loved all three. Marius called the fourth moon Ganymede, the name of a handsome young prince in Greek mythology. The moons' names are still in use today.

EXPLORING THE PLANET

Four centuries passed before scientists attempted a serious study of Jupiter. In the 1960s astronomers knew that our Solar System's largest planets were coming into alignment. This meant that the orbits of Jupiter, Saturn, Uranus, and Neptune would put them in line with each other. It was an ideal time to attempt a mission to all four planets. The alignment would start to fade by the end of the 1970s, and would not happen again for another 176 years.

The biggest challenge for scientists was to design a spacecraft that could reach all four planets before the alignment had ended. A University of California in Los Angeles graduate student named Michael Minovitch came up with a way to do just that. His plan was to use the gravity of each planet as a source of energy to power the spacecraft. The gravitational force would act like a slingshot, propelling the craft further along its way, at an increased speed. After visiting Neptune, the outermost planet, the craft would leave our Solar System forever and disappear into interstellar space. In 1965, another graduate student, Gary Flandro, came up with a slightly different plan. He called it the

Strong telescopes can be used to view Jupiter, but sometimes the giant planet can be seen in the night sky with the naked eye. In this photograph, Venus is at the top left, the Moon is in the center, and Jupiter is to the right.

"grand tour." Using the slingshot effect of each planet's gravity, a spacecraft would visit all four of the outer planets. However, at each stop it would conduct in-depth scientific research.

By 1971, a team of designers at the Jet Propulsion Laboratory in California had designed a spacecraft to do the job. It would be powered by **nuclear reactors** and would have five computers on board that could talk with each other and carry out commands on their own. The craft would also have an advanced communications system that could send back photos as well as information about the planets. However, NASA decided the design was too expensive and too complex. So the agency gave the contract to a competing team of designers. This other team put their heads together and came up with the first two spacecraft ever to visit Jupiter. They called their spacecraft *Pioneer 10* and *Pioneer 11*. The launch date was set for Thursday, March 2, 1972.

FIRST MISSIONS TO JUPITER: *PIONEER 10 AND 11*

In February both spacecraft were moved to the launch site at Cape Canaveral in Florida. Each one carried a gold-plated copper disk that contained images and sounds that would introduce our civilization to any extraterrestrial beings the spacecraft might come across. The images showed the location of Earth and included a pair of humans, male and female.

On March 2, *Pioneer 10* launched into space. On December 3, 1973, *Pioneer 10* came within 50,000 miles (81,000 km) of Jupiter's cloud tops. Even though the spacecraft did not have cameras, special instruments on board sent back images of this historic encounter. *Pioneer 10* was the first spacecraft to travel to the outer planets. It was also the first to pass through

Spacecraft like *Pioneer 10* and *Pioneer 11* are launched into space using powerful rockets.

the asteroid belt beyond Mars and the first to take close-up pictures of Jupiter. On June 13, 1983, it left our Solar System behind and raced onward into interstellar space. Nearly twenty years later, on January 23, 2003, *Pioneer 10* returned its last signal to Earth. By that time, it had traveled more than 7 billion miles (11.3 billion km) from our planet.

Pioneer 10's flyby of Jupiter was so successful that the design team decided the next mission should be even more daring. Engineers improved *Pioneer 11*'s instruments and planned to have the spacecraft head toward Saturn after flying past Jupiter. On April 5, 1973, *Pioneer 11* blasted off. On December 2, 1974, it came within 21,000 miles (34,000 km) of Jupiter's cloud tops.

Onboard scanners photographed the Great Red Spot as well as Jupiter's polar regions. Other instruments performed a range of scientific tests, which included analyzing Jupiter's atmosphere, auroras, and the planet's magnetic field. After completing its flyby, *Pioneer 11* streaked toward Saturn, reaching that planet in 1979. From Saturn, the spacecraft continued on a path that would eventually take it out of the Solar System. The last signal from *Pioneer 11* was received on September 30, 1995. Today, the location of *Pioneer 11* remains unknown.

Before *Pioneer 10* and *Pioneer 11*, astronomers really did not know much about Jupiter. Thanks to these missions, astronomers made several important discoveries, which included realizing that Jupiter probably does not have a solid core. If one exists, it could be made of liquid metallic hydrogen. The missions also determined that the atmosphere is a turbulent mix of ammonia, methane, and other gases. It was discovered that the Great Red Spot is a giant storm larger than the Earth. Without those two *Pioneer* missions, scientists would not have known that Jupiter generates its own heat.

VOYAGER 1 AND VOYAGER 2

Scientists and engineers at the Jet Propulsion Laboratory created a new set of spacecraft for the next missions to Jupiter. On August 20, 1977, *Voyager 2* took off for a tour of the four outer planets in our Solar System. One month later, *Voyager 1* was launched. Its flight path would take it past Titan, one of Saturn's moons. However, first, it would visit Jupiter. *Voyager 1* and *Voyager 2* reached Jupiter in 1979. Both spacecraft investigated Jupiter's four largest moons. The spacecraft provided scientists with a lot of information about the moons' characteristics.

In addition to making major discoveries about Jupiter's four outer moons, the *Voyager* spacecraft were the first to detect the planet's faint system of rings. The *Voyagers* also discovered three new moons—Adrastea and Metis, which lie outside Jupiter's rings, and Thebe, located between Io and the moon Amalthea, which had been discovered in 1892.

The *Voyager* missions were among the most successful in the history of space exploration. After completing their exploration of Jupiter, both spacecraft embarked for Saturn late in the summer of 1979.

This image of Callisto was taken by *Voyager 2* in 1979.

4

CURRENT AND FUTURE MISSIONS TO JUPITER

GALILEO

The *Galileo* spacecraft consisted of an **orbiter** and a probe. The major goals of the *Galileo* mission were to conduct long-term observations of Jupiter and study the four outer moons more closely than the *Voyagers* had done. On October 18, 1989, *Galileo* was launched, and six years later it reached Jupiter and began to orbit the giant planet. In July 1995, the *Galileo* probe began a five-month free fall toward the planet. It would

The *Galileo* spacecraft provided scientists with new information about Jupiter and new images of the planet.

be the first spacecraft ever to drop directly into Jupiter's deadly atmosphere. On December 7, the probe crashed into the top of the atmosphere at a speed of 106,000 miles (170,000 km) per hour. Once the probe slowed down, it released its parachute and opened its heat shield. For the next and final hour of its existence, the probe relayed a continuous stream of information. It showed that Jupiter's atmosphere was different from the Sun's. (Scientists had expected that both atmospheres would contain similar elements in similar quantities.) The probe measured

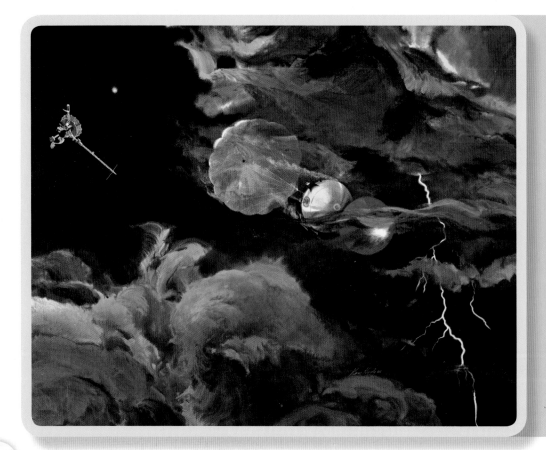

Galileo's probe (shown with the parachute) collected a great deal of information about Jupiter's atmosphere and lightning.

lightning bolts, which were up to one thousand times more powerful than lightning on Earth. The probe also discovered massive thunderstorms above and below Jupiter's equator. It also discovered clouds made from ammonia gas. Such clouds had never before been found in any planet's atmosphere.

After receiving the last transmission from the probe, the *Galileo* orbiter began its first orbit of Jupiter. By this time, extreme heat and pressure had destroyed the probe. But the information it had sent back would keep scientists busy for months to come. Over the next two years, the orbiter made eleven orbits around Jupiter and performed ten close flybys of Ganymede, Callisto, Io, and Europa. The orbiter came closer to the moons than either of the *Voyagers*. It flew so close to Europa, onboard cameras could see features the size of a school bus on the moon's surface. Flying past Io, the orbiter photographed a fountain of fire erupting.

Galileo's main mission ended in 1997, but its tremendous success inspired mission leaders to keep it going for another six years, until 2003. During its first extended mission (the *Galileo* Europa Mission), it found even more evidence of an ocean under Europa's icy crust. The orbiter also found signs that liquid saltwater may be under the frozen surfaces of Ganymede and Callisto, too. It showed that Ganymede has a magnetic field. Ganymede is the only moon in the Solar System that can generate its own magnetic field.

SHOEMAKER-LEVY 9

On March 23, 1993, three American astronomers discovered a comet orbiting Jupiter. It had probably been circling the Sun but then had been captured by Jupiter's gravity. When it flew too close to Jupiter, the planet's overwhelming gravitational force broke the comet up into smaller pieces. By the time the astronomers had spotted this comet, it consisted of twenty fragments lined up like pearls on a string.

The comet, called Shoemaker-Levy 9, was named after Carolyn and Eugene Shoemaker and David Levy, the astronomers who discovered it. They calculated that the fragments would smash into Jupiter's atmosphere in July 1994. This would be the first time in history that people would actually see a comet collide with a planet. The results of the impacts were amazing. Each one was like hundreds of nuclear bombs exploding. Fireballs from the explosions were up to 2,500 miles (4,023 km) wide. The explosions were so powerful they left black scorch marks in Jupiter's outer atmosphere. Some of these marks had diameters larger than Earth's. If one of those fragments had smashed into Earth, the blast would have left behind a crater the size of the state of Rhode Island.

Shoemaker-Levy 9's string-of-pearls appearance is shown in this 1994 photograph from NASA.

Galileo's other achievements include measuring the volcanic activity on Io. There are about one hundred times more eruptions on Io than there are on Earth. During one four-month period, the orbiter observed eruptions from the volcano Pillan on Io. The volcano spewed enough lava to cover an area the size of Arizona. *Galileo* also determined that Jupiter's rings are created from moon dust. On September 21, 2003, the *Galileo* orbiter began its descent into Jupiter's atmosphere. The orbiter's mission had come to a fiery end after a string of record-breaking achievements.

NEW HORIZONS

The *New Horizons* mission launched in January 2006. It is part of NASA's New Frontiers Program and is the first mission to Pluto. (Pluto used to be considered the ninth and outermost planet in the Solar System. However, because of its size, Pluto was reclassified as a dwarf planet in 2006.) One year after launch, the *New Horizons* spacecraft flew past Jupiter on its way to Pluto. This was the fastest trip to Jupiter ever made by a spacecraft launched from Earth. The craft's closest encounter with Jupiter took place on February 28, 2007. It came within 1.4 million miles (2.3 million km) of the planet.

For several weeks before and after this encounter, cameras on *New Horizons* took pictures of Jupiter and its four largest moons. The images are among the clearest and most detailed ever taken. They have given astronomers exciting new ways of seeing and understanding Jupiter's atmosphere, its moons and rings, and its magnetosphere. The images show the first close-ups of the Little Red Spot, a new storm on Jupiter that formed within the past decade when three smaller storms combined forces. The Little Red Spot is about the half the size of Jupiter's Great Red Spot and about 70 percent of Earth's diameter.

New Horizons also photographed Jupiter's rings. These images have helped scientists better understand how the rings are formed. The spacecraft also focused on Io's lava flows, glowing pockets of gas, and a giant dust plume from the volcano Tvashtar. The plume rose about 200 miles (300 km) into space. Using Jupiter's gravity to increase its speed, *New Horizons*

New Horizons transmitted this image of Jupiter (left), Io (center), and Ganymede (upper right). The image is so clear that the moons' shadows are visible on Jupiter.

Jupiter's Little Red Spot is sometimes called Red Spot Junior, but its official name is Oval BA. The two Red Spots are shown in white on this image of Jupiter from 2006.

reached 50,000 miles (80,000 km) per hour. At this speed, the spacecraft is expected to reach Pluto by the year 2015.

THE *JUNO* MISSION

Juno, the next mission to Jupiter and its moons, is scheduled to launch in August 2011. Like *New Horizons,* it is part of NASA's New Frontiers Program. Its main purpose is to learn more about the origins and structure of the planet. Scientists believe that Jupiter has much to teach us about how our Solar System formed and evolved. The *Juno* spacecraft will attempt to look

Like Jupiter, the spacecraft *Juno* gets its name from Roman mythology. Juno was Jupiter's wife, the queen of the gods.

beneath the planet's colorful cloud cover and reveal the many secrets these clouds keep hidden.

If all goes according to plan, *Juno* will reach Jupiter in 2016 after a five-year journey. Then it will begin a series of thirty-two elliptical orbits around the planet's poles. The solar-powered craft will carry a variety of scientific instruments. Special instruments will probe beneath the clouds and measure energy coming from the planet's interior. These measurements will hopefully give scientists a much deeper understanding of Jupiter's composition and even its origins. Other instruments will study Jupiter's gravitational field and magnetosphere. Data from these studies may explain how Jupiter creates such dazzling auroras around its poles. This information may also reveal the mysterious structure of a planet that is mostly made of hydrogen and helium gas. Students who take part in the *Juno* Education and Public Outreach program will be able to view the first images of Jupiter's North Pole. The mission's JunoCam camera will begin sending back these images when the spacecraft reaches Jupiter in 2016.

IS THERE LIFE ON JUPITER?

It is very unlikely that any future space probes will find signs of life on Jupiter. Conditions on the planet are extremely harsh. If there is life, it would probably be airborne. The upper layers of the atmosphere have mild temperatures and tolerable atmospheric pressure and might support some primitive forms of life.

When it comes to Jupiter's moons, however, scientists tell a much different story. Volcanic Io is not a very suitable environment for living things, but scientists think the other three Galilean moons might contain life. The Galileo orbiter found very strong evidence of liquid water on these moons, and living things need water to survive.

Europa is the smallest of the Galilean moons. It is about the size of our own Moon. But unlike our Moon, Europa has a salt-water ocean beneath its icy crust. So far, this moon appears to be the most likely place to look for life among the many celestial

Future missions to Jupiter and its moons may one day reveal how life—maybe even human life—can survive on or near this fifth planet from the Sun.

Though Jupiter most likely cannot sustain life, Ganymede, one of its larger moons, may have the necessary water and warmth.

bodies that orbit Jupiter. Callisto and Ganymede might also harbor life. All three moons have bitter cold, frozen exteriors. However, their interiors could be warm enough for life to emerge.

It may be hard to imagine anything living on the moons of Jupiter. Even though at least three of them may have large amounts of liquid water, they are nothing like our Earth, where life is diverse and abundant. Most living things on Earth need sunlight in order to survive. But in recent years, scientists have discovered life-forms living in extremely harsh places right here on our own planet. For example, microorganisms called bacteria have been found at the bottom of the ocean near volcanic openings. Simple organisms have also been found in boiling hot water springs and even deep underground where there is no oxygen or sunlight.

Future missions to Jupiter will probably take a long, hard look at the moons of this giant planet. One of them may turn out to be the home of the first forms of extraterrestrial life ever discovered in our Solar System!

QUICK FACTS ABOUT JUPITER

ORIGIN OF THE PLANET'S NAME: Named after the king of the gods in Roman mythology.

DISCOVERY: Known since ancient times, but Jupiter's four largest moons were discovered in 1610 by the Italian astronomer Galileo.

SIZE: 88,846 miles (142,984 km) in diameter at the equator.

DISTANCE FROM EARTH: About 391 million miles (629 million km) to 577 million miles (929 million km).

DISTANCE FROM SUN: About 483.8 million miles (778.6 million km).

LENGTH OF YEAR: 11.86 Earth years

LENGTH OF DAY: About 10 Earth hours

NUMBER OF MOONS: 49 named and 14 numbered. The largest moons are Ganymede, Io, Callisto, and Europa.

RINGS: A series of three faint and narrow rings made of dust particles from Jupiter's inner moons.

COMPOSITION: Mostly gas and liquid hydrogen with a dense core that may be made of rock and ice.

ATMOSPHERE: Mostly hydrogen and helium with small amounts of methane, ammonia, water, hydrocarbons, and other gases.

GLOSSARY

asteroid—A small, rocky object orbiting the Sun. Most asteroids can be found in the asteroid belt between Mars and Jupiter. Many asteroids are fragments of destroyed planets. Others form from the raw material that goes into making a complete planet.

atom—The smallest building block of all matter.

aurora —A colorful display of light around a planet's poles. Auroras are caused by the interaction between atmospheric gases and electrically charged particles, usually from the Sun.

axis —An imaginary straight line going through a planet, around which the planet rotates.

comet—An object in the Solar System made mostly of ice and dust that did not become part of a planet's formation. Sometimes referred to as "dirty snowballs," comets have a solid part called the nucleus and a dust tail that can stretch for millions of miles. Comets are only visible when they come close to the Sun.

flyby—A space flight that travels close to a planet or moon for the purpose of making observations.

geology—The study of a planet's rocks, natural structures, and the processes and forces that shaped them.

gossamer—Jupiter's very faint, outermost dust ring.

gravity—The force between objects that makes them attract each other. The force of gravity increases as objects come closer together and decreases the farther apart they are.

halo—A thin, inner dust ring around Jupiter.

magnetosphere—The space around a planet in which the planet's magnetic field acts like a shield or protective bubble. The magnetosphere screens the planet from the solar wind, a constantly streaming flow of charged particles from the Sun. Jupiter's magnetosphere is the largest object in the Solar System.

mantle—The region of Earth or another planet that is located between the core and the outer crust.

meteorite—A chunk of rock from outer space that has passed through Earth's atmosphere and landed on Earth.

nuclear reactors—Energy-creating devices that use nuclear reactions for power. A nuclear reaction is a process in which huge amounts of energy are released either by splitting atoms or by fusing them together. Nuclear fusion reactions are what happen in the cores of stars, like our Sun.

orbit—The path taken by a celestial body, such as a planet or a moon.

orbiter—A spacecraft that orbits a planet or a moon in the Solar System.

probe—Any kind of spacecraft designed to explore extraterrestrial objects and send back data to computers on Earth.

satellites—Any natural or human-made object that orbits a larger body such as a planet or a moon.

solar wind—A steady stream of electrically charged particles from the Sun's atmosphere.

Solar System—The Sun and all the orbiting objects around it.

terrestrial—Relating to land rather than to the sea or atmosphere.

FIND OUT MORE

BOOKS

Bortz, Fred. *Beyond Jupiter: The Story of Planetary Astronomer Heidi Hammel.* New York: Franklin Watts, 2005.

Feinstein, Stephen. *Jupiter.* Berkeley Heights, NJ: Enslow Publishers, 2005.

Goss, Tim. *Jupiter.* Chicago: Heinemann Library, 2008.

Slade, Suzanne. *A Look at Jupiter.* New York: PowerKids Press, 2008.

WEBSITES

Ask an Astronomer
http://curious.astro.cornell.edu/index.php

CoolCosmos: Jupiter
http://coolcosmos.ipac.caltech.edu/cosmic_kids/AskKids/jupiter.shtml

The Discovery of the Galilean Satellites
http://www2.jpl.nasa.gov/galileo/ganymede/discovery.html

Discovery of Jupiter
http://www.windows.ucar.edu/tour/link=/jupiter/discovery.html&edu=high

JUNO
http://juno.wisc.edu/mission.html

Jupiter
http://kids.nineplanets.org/jupiter.htm

NASA Kids' Club
http://www.nasa.gov/audience/forkids/kidsclub/flash/index.html

The Satellites of Jupiter
http://galileo.rice.edu/sci/observations/jupiter_satellites.html

BIBLIOGRAPHY

The author found these references especially helpful while researching this book.

Corfield, Richard. *Lives of the Planets.* New York: Basic Books, 2007.

Harman, William K. and Ron Miller. *The Grand Tour (A Traveler's Guide to the Solar System).* New York: Workman Publishing Company, 2005.

Jupiter: Gas Giant. http://www2.jpl.nasa.gov/galileo/jupiter/jupiter.html

Lin, Douglas N. C. "The Genesis of the Planets." http://www.sciam.com/article.cfm?id=the-genesis-of-planets

The Magnetic Field of Jupiter. http://csep10.phys.utk.edu/astr161/lect/jupiter/magnetic.html

NASA's New Frontiers Mission to Jupiter: JUNO. http://juno.wisc.edu/mission_pastmissions.html

NASA. "Jupiter Ahoy!" http://pluto.jhuapl.edu/news_center/news/092606.html

---. World Book, "Jupiter." http://www1.nasa.gov/worldbook/jupiter_worldbook.html

New Horizons: NASA's Pluto—Kuiper Belt Mission. http://pluto.jhuapl.edu/news_center/news/092606.html

Solar System Exploration. http://solarsystem.nasa.gov/planets/profile.cfm?Object=Jupiter&Display=Moons

Welcome to the Planets. http://pds.jpl.nasa.gov/planets/welcome/jupiter.htm

INDEX

ABOUT THE AUTHOR

When George Capaccio was around ten years old, he started getting interested in outer space. He talked his father into putting up bedroom wallpaper that was covered with rocket ships and stars and planets. He even had carpet that had space designs, and built model rocket ships, which he hung from the ceiling. Nowadays, he makes his living as a writer and storyteller for children. Every now and then he manages to find time for a trip to one of his favorite planets—in his imagination, of course.